The Ottoman Harem

in the 19th Century

D1654261

İstanbul 2013

This is a TBMM National Palaces publication.
All publishing rights are reserved.
Publication No. 89

Published on behalf of National Palaces by
Dr. Yasin Yıldız
TBMM Asst. General Secretary (National Palaces)

Editorial Board
Dr. Kemal Kahraman
Asst. Prof. Dr. Bülent Arı
Dr. Halil İbrahim Erbay
İlhan Kocaman
Dr. Jale Beşkonaklı
Şule Gürbüz
T. Cengiz Göncü

Text
Summarized from the
National Palaces publication
"Harem ve Cariyelik"
prepared by T. Cengiz Göncü.

Editor
Dr. İlona Baytar

Art Director
Esin Öncü

Photography
Suat Alkan

Translation
Aişe Aslı Sancar

Acknowledgment
Gökşen Canıyılmaz
Çağla Parlak
Nurdan Yalçın

Front and Back Covers
Osman Hamdi, A Young Girl Having Her Hair Combed,
detail, oil on canvas, 39 x 58 cm, National Palaces Collection.

Printed By
Görsel Dizayn Ofset Matbaacılık Tic. Ltd. Şti.
Atatürk Bulvarı Deposite Alışveriş Merkezi A5 Blok
4. Kat No: 405 İkitelli OSB - Başakşehir / İstanbul
Tel: 0212 671 91 00
Sertifika No: 16269

ISBN 978-605-4700-45-5

Contents

Foreword

In addition to protecting the material existence of palaces, kiosks and pavilions, the National Palaces has adopted as a basic principle the exposition of the rich historical and cultural heritage surrounding these structures. Within this framework, shedding light on all aspects of 19th century palace life carries great importance.

Heading the list on topics of interest regarding palace life is the Imperial Harem, which symbolizes the private lives of Ottoman rulers and their families. Developing within a historical process, the Orientalist discourse diverted the real meanings of harem and the institution of jariyes (slave women) to a very different foundation, and it presented these concepts as a "symbol of worldly pleasures" peculiar to Eastern societies.

In this small book, evaluations have been made to the effect that the Imperial Harem was an important part of the politics of the Ottoman state and dynasty. Views of harem chambers in the Dolmabahçe Palace, which reflects the most ideal palace shape in the Reform Period, and living spaces of Ottoman rulers and family members have been put forth with all their authenticity.

I hope that this small book, which takes up the Ottoman Harem and the institution of jariyes on a scientific basis, will make a great contribution to our cultural life and I thank all my colleagues who participated in the preparation of this work.

Cemil ÇİÇEK
Speaker of the Grand National Assembly

The Ottoman Harem

Beyond being the name of an establishment, the Imperial Harem, which is a unit connected to the Imperial Mabeyn Chambers (Selamlık) within the Ottoman palace structure, finds its expression both architecturally and abstractly. While as a physical structure, the Imperial Harem represents the space closed to the outside where the sultan, family members and the jariyes who served them lived, when its architecture is examined, it can be seen that this space reflects all the traces of Ottoman palace organization, protocol and customs. On the other hand, however, the abstract meaning of "harem" and the "Imperial Harem" are usually overlooked. It is thought that the harem, in relation to the Ottoman palace, is just the special section of the palace designated for women. However, this concept includes the private lives of the sultanate family, beginning with the sultan himself, their interpersonal relationships, and a private space not shared with the outer world. The concept of the jariye institution is another concept associated with the Imperial Harem. Of great importance because it is an institution that provides the basic human resources for the Imperial Harem, the jariye system has taken on different meanings than its real meaning throughout the historical process.

Dolmabahçe Palace, The central hall of the Sultan's Chamber (Blue Hall).

The Harem and the Imperial Harem

With its root "haramu(m)" meaning "to cover, to hide, to conceal from others, to separate, to isolate," the word "harem" in Arabic means "a protected, sacred and honored thing or place." In the classic Ottoman Turkish house, the name "harem" was given to the division of the home reserved for the family which was usually planned so as to look at the inner courtyard and where women could comfortably live their daily lives without encountering male strangers.

In the palace, which had the appearance of a large Turkish house, the "selamlık" section which was open to the outside world was followed by the private section also called the "harem" where the master of the house and family members lived. Together with the sultan's private space being call "Darûssaâde" (Abode of Happiness) in Ottoman tradition, the terms "harem" and the "Imperial Harem" were widely used.

The harem was a section "closed to strangers". In addition to the harem sections in all palaces during the classic and modern periods being protected by sound ramparts, walls or doors and locks made from the heaviest iron, the women living sequestered lives, their seclusion when they left their homes and their giving importance to privacy all made the harem mysterious. The difficulty of reaching the harem and harem life caused those who could not enter this space to use their imaginations. The imaginary descriptions written by foreign travelers, ambassadors and slaves who had worked in harems were presented as real in the Western world and they were perceived that way as well. The observations of Grace Ellison, who had been in distinguished Ottoman harems at the beginning of the 20th century and who had analyzed social life, can be considered to be an example of how a cautious approach is required for far from objective discourses related to the Imperial Harem:

"A Turkish man is in love with his home and his wife. He is a tolerant husband and a courteous father. When the West reads something in relation to the houses of Easterners, they expect to hear distorted stories. This incorrect information about what is going on beyond closed doors is given an ugly shape, spirit and spread by governesses who have been fired from their jobs and ladies from Pera who are rarely distinguished with an opportunity to go inside."

John Frederick Lewis, *From Harem*, 1873, detail, oil on canvas, 62.5 x 70 cm, (Osmanlı Sarayı'nda Oryantalistler, p. 22).

Jariyes

When the harem is considered, one of the most important concepts brought to mind is "jariye". Used for every kind of female slave, jariye is a general term describing the servant class of the palace. The institution of the jariye had an important place in the Imperial Harem and it provided basic human resources at the same time. The term jariye calls up the widespread belief that each slave in the palace was a wife of the sultan, it was usually used as a vehicle for a negative view of the structure of the Ottoman sultanate and more generally of Turkish-Islamic culture and civilization. Generally this approach accepted the Western descriptions of the harem and jariye instead of seeking and researching the truth.

Actually, the jariye concept is directly related to the implementation of slavery. The enslavement of some people by others and slavery as a system was a general legal principle in all legal systems and religions throughout the history of mankind. It was practiced in all known societies and cultures like in ancient India, China, Egypt, Mesopotamia, Greece, Rome, Jewish society and pre-Islamic Arab society. There were advocates of slavery practiced in antiquity and ancient civilizations. In his work entitled, *Politics*, the Greek philosopher Aristotle tried to prove that "slavery is both natural and legitimate". Since the time of the Old Testament, all monotheistic religions approved of slavery and tried to soften its strict applications. With the advent of Islam, slavery was seen as necessary for social life and the economy; there was not much thought to the contrary, but

Pierre Désiré Guillemet, *Lady from the Palace*, 1875, detail, oil on canvas, 97 x 77.5 cm, National Palaces Collection.

new arrangements related to slavery were made. Absolute abolishment of slavery was only possible with a change of paradigm on this subject by the international community. Islamic law indicated that slaves were human beings, that it was necessary to treat them humanely, and that they had rights as human beings before the law. When machines became more common after the Industrial Revolution in the West, the need for slaves decreased and an attempt was made to abolish slavery.

A palace woman, (Bahattin Öztuncay, Hanedan ve Kamera).

As a result of the approach to the practice of slavery brought by Islam, the employment of slaves in Ottoman society was different from the understanding in the West. In fact, one of the most important reasons for most slaves and jariyes' refusal of emancipation and the choice of their own free will to remain living with their masters was as foreign observers stated, "In Ottoman society a slave is seen as a servant and is treated as a member of the household." Parallel to the practice in Ottoman society, jariyes also possessed an important place in the palace. So much so that the women in highest ranks in the hierarchy of the Imperial Harem -valide sultan and wife of the sultan- were chosen from among jariyes. Regarding the practice of slavery in the Islamic world, Alphonse de Lamartine wrote in his work, *Voyage en Orient*:

Hürrem Sultan, the wife of Suleiman the Magnificent, (A. V. Schweiger, Die Frauen Des Orients, Dolmabahçe Palace Caliph Abdülmecid Library).

"I witnessed two or three deeds of mercy of devout Muslims that would even make Christian compassion envious. Several Turks bought and took some elderly jariyes who had been sold by their masters because of their advanced age and handicap. I asked of what benefit those poor women could be. The slave trader replied to me, 'They will gain God's approval for these men.' I learned from my guide Mr. Morlac that many Muslim Turks send their men to the bazaar to buy handicapped male slaves and jariyes to feed them in their homes as a good deed. I guess God's presence does not leave these people."

Representing a service class and coming from the institution of slavery, jariyes not only refer to a service class unique to the sultan's chamber. There were always jariyes in the retinue of the valide sultan, the wives of the sultan, the daughters of the sultan and young princes. In fact, just as provisions were given to a prince or princess, a jariye was also given them and was called daye kalfa and dadı kalfa (meaning nurse). In addition, while mentioning any woman from his subjects other than the women in his harem, the sultan could use the term jariye. In petitions written by the daughters of the sultan, his sisters and the wives of deceased sultans, the women refer to themselves as "your jariye."

Parallels between the Pages and the Jariye Systems

There were similarities between the organization of the jariyes, who played a determining role in the formation of the Ottoman royal family, and the organization of the pages at the Third Courtyard. It has been determined that there were similarities between the organizations of the pages who were recruited and educated at the Enderun palace school and the jariyes who were brought to the

Imperial Harem by similar means, and that like in recruiting, the jariye institution functioned within a certain system and government policy. In both practices these basic principles were given priority: breaking the tie with the individual's roots, high and absolute loyalty, a humble attitude and behavior, immediate sacrifice of life when the continuity of the state and sultanate were at stake. Just as the sultan's authority was represented by state officials with their roots in the Janissary guards, harem etiquette and culture were transferred to social life by means of the jariyes.

The upper mobility from the lowest ranks of the jariyes in the Imperial Harem to the highest level of stewardesses (excluding the stations of the sultan's favorites and the valide sultan) shows many similarities in many respects to the Enderun organization's promotion system. Just as recruited male children were trained in the army, Enderun school and rose in the ranks of the military and bureaucratic elite of the Ottoman Empire, jariyes taken into the harem rose to administrative positions like kalfa and usta according to their beauty and intelligence or, taking their rank as valide sultan and wife of the sultan, they succeeded in rising to the highest positions.

Like in the organizational structures of the jariyes and pages, there were also similarities in the dress of the two groups. While installing the organ presented as a gift by Queen Elizabeth in 1599 in the palace, British Thomas Dallam secretly watched the jariyes play ball; according to him, the women wore outfits similar to the pages and it was difficult to distinguish between the two.

The Ethnic Roots of the Jariyes and their Entrance into the Palace

Generally young girls were bought by ladies of İstanbul's large harems; they were carefully raised, trained with the etiquette of the elite class and then several years later sold to the sultan's harem or other large harems. Eunuchs who were members of these harems also participated in this kind of trade. When a jariye was being sold, her approval would be sought; she would not be sold against her will. If after the sale she was not pleased with her master's treatment, she had the right to request to be sold again.

Jariyes chosen for the palace in the 19th century were generally Circassian. The important reason for this was that as a result of the policy of dispersion practiced by Russians in Circassia, there were Circassian displaced persons who took refuge in the Ottoman state. Circassian immigrant families gave their children to the palace or rich mansions frequently of their own will at a designated price; the purpose of this was not to earn a profit from their children, but to enable their children to have a better life and to gain status. It is known that while Circassians raised their daughters, they dreamed about them one day becoming jariyes in the Ottoman palace or a wealthy family's mansion. To separate Circassian jariyes from North African slaves, they were called "white jariyes." Just as buying jariyes for the palace was a means of procuring them, it was also a widespread custom to give them as a gift to the palace. State officials and members of the royal family also procured jariyes for

Pierre Désiré Guillemet, *Lady from the Palace*, 1874, detail, oil on canvas, 98 x 79 cm, National Palaces Collection.

the palace. The valide sultan, in particular, gave attention to this matter. In the mid-19th century when buying and selling slaves was prohibited among the Ottomans, Circassians continued to give their daughters to the palace of their own free will.

Jariyes who performed duty in the final period of the Ottoman palace mention in their memoirs that Circassian jariyes had different status according to their regions. According to this, Circassians were family members of poor farmers, Abhazes were from the elite and noble, Georgians were from middle-class families. While Circassian girls were in the majority during Sultan Abdülmecid's reign, beginning with Sultan Abdülaziz's reign, Abhaz girls took priority.

Another source of jariye procurement for the harem was state officials sending them as a gift to the sultan. Jariyes raised or bought by the grand vizier, in particular,

The anteroom of the Valide Sultan Chamber in the Harem of the Dolmabahçe Palace (Pink Hall).

Harem in the 19th Century, (A. V. Schweiger, Die Frauen Des Orients).

the members of the state council, governors, governors of sancaks (sub-divisions of provinces), and the sultan's sisters were presented to the sultan. While this was seen more frequently during the reigns of Murad III, Abdülmecid and Abdülmecid II, governors giving jariyes as gifts continued until the last century. When jariyes who entered the palace by this means became a favorite of the sultan or valide sultan, she would become the patron of the state official who presented her as a gift and would make political cooperation when necessary.

The most important person supervising the procurement of jariyes for the palace or, if necessary, procuring them personally was undoubtedly the valide sultan. It has been established that until the final years of the reign of Sultan Abdülaziz, Pertevniyal Valide Sultan bought Circassian jariyes for the palace. The jariyes the valide sultan chose or personally oversaw the purchase of were either employed in the most important chambers in the harem or were given as gifts to state officials.

During the reign of Sultan Abdülaziz another person who played a role in the procurement of well-trained jariyes was Tiryal Hanım, one of the wives of the sultan's father, Sultan Mahmud II, and a virtual second mother to Sultan Abdülaziz. The Darûssaâde Aghas and the eunuchs under their administration in the palace acted as intermediaries for procurement of jariyes for the palace and distinguished mansions.

In the receipts which documented that slave traders who sold the jariyes had gotten their fee and which were made out in the presence of witnesses, it was recorded that the purchase was made with the approval of the parties (seller, jariye and guardian), the jariye was free of illness, her age and that she was Circassian. The seller indicated that the jariye was his possession. With this, the legitimacy of the sale was documented, and the exchange was termed a "sale (furuht)".

It was stated on the receipt that the seller would have no right to make a claim on the jariye in the future and that the jariye was not free; it was indicated that if a contrary situation arose, the money would have to be refunded. When records of sales for the years 1874-75 were examined, it was found that the age of the jariyes was from 8-18, they were sold for between 35 and 130 lira, the jariye trade was made mostly by Circassian traders, and some of these were Circassian immigrants. It was also determined that some harem aghas and gentlemen-in-waiting to the sultan who had been manumitted directly sold jariyes to the valide sultan.

Royal Policy and the Selection of the Sultan's Wives

The sultan's wives were chosen as Christians in the 14th century and from among Muslim women in the 15th century. (This change in the 15th century reflects the increasing importance of the Ottomans in Anatolia.) After the first half of the 15th century with both the disappearance of neighboring states of the Ottomans or principalities and the decrease in political benefit of marriage ties with other dynasties, marriage among royal families began to cease and jariyes were given preference. The preference for jariyes shows parallelism with recruits gaining more weight in state administrative levels. In other words, the "harem" and "jariye" institutions made as a result of conscious dynastic policy are closely tied to Ottoman political structure and sultanate politics.

Sultans choosing wives from among jariyes is an historical phenomenon. However, to claim that the sultan had intimate relations with all the jariyes living in the harem, the number of which reached 500-600 during the second half of the 19th century, does not correspond to historical fact. The sultan had a marital relationship with only a few among the hundreds of jariyes; he was not in contact with the rest. Ottoman sultans were very reserved and acted on a very high level with the jariyes who served them. In her memoirs Ayşe Osmanoğlu states that her father, Sultan Abdülhamid II, used the polite form of Turkish when he addressed the jariyes who served him.

The relationship between a jariye with the status of servant and her master was just a work relationship. Jariyes in this status served in her master's eating, drinking, cleanliness or other tasks. This is indicated by their being called by the names of Ewer Stewardess, Coffee Stewardess, Pantry Stewardess and similar titles.

According to their seniority and rank, jariyes were separated into categories like high officials, first class, second class, third class, fourth class, caregivers for the sick, cooks, and stokers of the bath. Princesses and wives of the sultan were mentioned as "devletlû, ismetlû" (excellent and virtuous); jariyes were referred to as "cevârî-i iffetsimât" or "cevârî-i iffetşiâr" (jariyes of chaste qualities and jariyes of chaste traits). While this description distinguished members of the dynasty from women who were not members, it also emphasized that the women in the Caliph's harem were concrete embodiments of the concepts of purity, innocence and chastity.

Just as the women carrying the title of wife or favorite could come from the ranks of the palace's service class, they could also be chosen from those who entered the palace as gifts or were bought for the palace. Wives whose sons took the throne took the title valide sultan and their rank was superior to the wives of the sultan in all periods. They

1 Müşfika Kadın Efendi, Fourth Wife of Sultan Abdülhamid II, (Harun Açba, Kadınefendiler).

2 Kamures Kadın Efendi, Senior Wife of Sultan Mehmed (Reşad) V, (Harun Açba, Kadınefendiler).

3 Mihrengiz Kadın Efendi, Second Wife of Sultan Mehmed (Reşad) V, (Harun Açba, Kadınefendiler).

4 Nazperver Kadın Efendi, Third Wife of Mehmed (Reşad) V, (Harun Açba, Kadınefendiler).

not only gave attention to the administration of the harem, but from time to time they intervened in government work; this was seen by their correspondence with some state officials. In the same way, it is also known that mothers of the sultans regularly gave aid to religious institutions, schools the poor and that they undertook building activities like the construction of fountains, mosques, and schools.

General Information Regarding Jariyes

Numbers, Salaries and Provisions

Like all members of the Imperial Harem, jariyes also had their own hierarchy. Generally they were separated into the three main classes of novice, kalfa (assistant stewardess) and usta (stewardess). Upon entering the palace, a jariye first would be registered in a corps notebook and then Persian palace names would be given which usually mentioned the girl's physical or personal traits. In their training, novices first were taught to read and write Turkish, rules of palace etiquette and some branches of the fine arts. Jariyes who passed basic training would then begin service in the chambers with the kalfas.

After 7-9 years of service, the jariyes were either promoted or manumitted. Those promoted would take the title "kalfa". The real weight of the palace was on the kalfas and they were personally responsible for the training of novice jariyes. Kalfas followed above the class of novices among the jariye staff in the palace; the usta class was a rank above these. One of the ustas, the treasury stewardess, was at the head of all of the jariyes in the Imperial Harem, and the valide sultan managed the harem with the skills of the ustas. While there were jariyes in the rank of usta among the jariyes of the sultan, the valide sultan, the princes and the princesses, records show that there were no jariyes of this rank among the jariyes serving the sultan's wives and favorites, who had no blood ties to the royal family. This indicates that

John Frederick Lewis, *Harem Life*, İstanbul, 1857, detail, watercolors, 61.2 x 48.1 cm, (Doğu'nun Cazibesi Britanya Oryantalist Resmi, p. 251).

Guiseppe Aureli, *From the Harem*, detail, oil paint on canvas, 33 x 47 cm, (Oryantalistlerin İstanbulu, p. 149).

only members of the royal family could have jariyes with the rank of usta in their services.

The hierarchy and number of jariyes in the service of two Reform Period sultans, Sultan Abdülmecid and Sultan Abdülaziz, were determined in light of some stipend and provisions registers belonging to the Imperial Harem; the number of jariyes which ranged between 500 and 600 were shown in the following way: 18 treasury stewardesses are recorded under the title "treasurers." They are followed by 22 high-ranking kalfas. There are 9 ustas in the first class, 8 kalfas in the second class, and 67 third-class kalfas. The fourth class, the most crowded one, was comprised of 365 novices. After these there are kalfas in various services: 15 pantry kalfas, 9 bath stoker kalfas, 17 medical kalfas, 44 jariyes in the chamber of the crown prince, 100 in the chamber of the valide sultan, 242 in the chambers of the princes and princesses, 99 in the chambers of the wives and favorites, and 29 jariyes in the chamber of the mother of Crown Prince Abdülaziz Efendi.

In addition, the presence of a head bather and second bather, 1 fumigator, 4 female doctors, and 4 midwives were established. According to the findings, the governess was at the top of the hierarchy in the chambers of the princes and princesses, followed by the wet nurse and the other kalfas. While the head kalfa was at the summit of the staff in the chambers of the sultan's wives and favorites, some of the jariyes in the staffs of the valide sultan and mature princes and princesses were called ustas. From the time the jariyes were admitted to the palace, they were allocated salaries and provisions (clothing, food, etc.). While salaries were given as daily stipends before the Reform Period, they were given on a monthly basis beginning with the Reform Period. In addition to salaries, jariyes were given a stipend once a year called "muharremiye" (a gift given at the Muslim New Year). Although it is written in memoirs that the jariyes lived comfortably after they were manumitted with their accumulated salaries and gifts given to them, there were also those, especially towards the end of the sultanate, who were writhing in need and had to ask for help from the palace.

When a jariye or harem agha died, their possessions would return to their master, or in other words, a princess. Even if they had been freed and married, palace furnishings remained with the palace. Upon the death of jariyes without heirs, their estates would be determined by the Ministry of the Imperial Treasury related to Inheritance, and spent in places compatible with the sultan's will.

Harem Entertainment

In the harem where every action was tied to a rule and where a tight discipline was maintained, entertainment was awaited with great expectation. The sultan would announce with an imperial decree that an entertainment would be arranged, and this would initiate a period of intense preparation. Entertainment events also took place in the Royal Gardens of palaces like the Çırağan, Yıldız, and Beşiktaş palaces. This tradition continued until the end of the empire.

Music in the harem continued as a tradition from former Turkish states, particularly the palace harems of the Seljuks and had an important place from the beginning. Famous musical masters of the time gave lessons to talented jariyes with beautiful voices; in addition, there were instrumental and vocal groups of musicians comprised of jariyes from the palaces. Usually the musicians playing instruments rose to the rank of kalfa. Music lessons were given in the harem in the school of music and sometimes jariyes were sent to the houses of famous composers. Together with Westernization in the 19th century, playing the mandolin and piano became fashionable.

A music room was always established just next to the harem chambers. In the two largest palaces of the 19th century, the Çırağan and Dolmabahçe palaces, a chamber near the Mabeyn on the ground floor was used as a music room. There was a Western music orchestra formed from jariyes in the palace harem during the Reform Period. The band and orchestra practiced twice a week and the instrumental group practiced once a week; dancing girls practiced in another room and

Fornari, *Woman Playing String Instrument*, detail, watercolors on paper, 33 x 23.5 cm, (Osmanlı Topraklarında İtalyan Oryantalistler, p. 245).

Guest Hall No. 163 in the Dolmabahçe Palace Harem where ceremonies and entertainment were arranged. The dowries of Sultan Abdülmecid's daughters, Cemile and Münire Sultan, were also displayed in this hall.

they would play all together in the anteroom on practice days.

These intelligent and talented girls were skillful enough to each play several musical instruments. Music would be performed in the large guest hall in the harem section of the Dolmabahçe Palace. This hall would be heated by braziers during the winter. Young princesses and princes attended this kind of entertainment, but, as an old palace custom, mature princes could not attend these group events on formal days.

The sultans personally supported the jariyes' art of dancing along with their singing and playing musical instruments. Sultans Mahmud II and Abdülmecid's coming to watch performances made by jariyes in the harem on certain days of the week was support for them on the highest level. Leyla Saz describes the instrumental nights attended by Sultan Abdülmecid as follows:

"Wives of the sultan (kadın efendi and Ikbals) would gather in the music hall and wait for the sultan; when the second treasury stewardess was seen, everyone stood up and got into line. When Sultan Abdülmecid entered, all bowed down to the floor and gave the Turkish salute. The Sultan would complement them saying, 'I am happy to listen to the music together; God's will we will enjoy it.'"

Sultan Abdülhamid II frequently listened to a small orchestra comprised of piano, violin and string instruments performed by jariyes in the palace.

Manumission of Jariyes

The length of service of a jariye was between 7 and 9 years. A master who did not free his jariye after this period of time was seen to be blameworthy. Devout and benevolent masters in long-established and large families kept their jariyes for shorter terms and then manumitted them. Jariyes who did not accept their freedom although they had been manumitted by their masters were still given a document of manumission and the decision as to when to leave was left up to them. The same practice was in force for jariyes in the palace.

Asking for release by jariyes and kalfas was considered shameful because it meant being tired of the palace. For this reason, jariyes who wanted to be released from service expressed this desire in a well-mannered way. If one of the jariyes wanted to leave, no one would want to be a vehicle for this and the princess or wife who was being served by the jariye would not make any requests on this matter. In this situation, jariyes would find an opportunity to enter their mistress' room without being seen; they would either put their petition next to a pillow or someplace it could be seen and then they would isolate themselves in their room. A kalfa who wanted to leave her service duty would write on a large piece of paper on holy days, "your slave seeks a goal, benefaction is her master's," and then sign the paper and leave it in an easily seen place; then she would stay in her room so as not to be seen by her master again.

She would not serve again before she left, she would not put in a general appearance and she would never appear before her mistress. Kalfas who wanted to help the jariye would support her and, in a sense, make propaganda for her. Sometimes months and years would pass; in fact some waited for as long as five years. Sometimes the jariye would grow weary of waiting in her room or her friends would convince her to change her mind and renounce her request. In regard to those whose request to leave was accepted, their masters would have their dowries made, give them money and send them to the house of a former slave. When a suitable match was found, the jariye would be married.

According to palace custom, if a jariye requested to leave service and marry someone from the city, (even if she was a favorite) as long as she was not pregnant, her request would be accepted.

Palace Women

In order for the secrets of the harem not to be carried outside, jariyes who were in the status of workers were usually not permitted to marry before they left the palace. Marrying palace women was popular in the provinces. Jariyes of the service or administrative class who were released from the palace and married were called "saraylı" or palace women and most of them continued their lives in neighborhoods close to the palace.

It is understood from the petitions of palace women presented to the imperial palace that after jariyes who were raised from childhood in the palace were released and married, their material and spiritual ties with the palace were not broken off.

Palace women were conveyors of social life, palace manners and culture. It has been concluded that women who spent the wealth they had accumulated at the palace for good works faced material difficulties at the beginning of the 20th century when the empire began to fall apart and economic balances began to deteriorate. For this reason they petitioned the palace for help. The continuation of the ties of manumitted jariyes with the palace throughout their lives and these women behaving like representatives of the palace are proof that the jariye system was a successful institution. Some of the jariyes manumitted from the palace passed their lives in places far from the sultanate like in Egypt, Damascus and the Hejaz; their salaries would be sent to them there by the Imperial Treasury.

Sandor Alexander Swoboda, *Palace Woman*, oil on canvas, 85.5 x 112 cm, National Palaces Collection.

In addition to those who were manumitted and married, there were also those who wanted to remain at the palace for the rest of their lives. When the Caliphate was abolished (March 3, 1924), it was found that in the New Chambers of the Dolmabahçe Palace there was an elderly jariye named Nazlı Melek Hanım who had been the chief clerk of the harem since the reign of Sultan Abdülmecid (approximately 60-70 years).

Hierarchy in the Harem

1. Novices

New slave girls in the Imperial Harem were called acemi (novice). Recruiting girls for the palace was just like recruiting Christian children from villages during the classical period. It has been determined that the children of Circassian families were given to the palace with their own approval. In this kind of exchange, a document made before witnesses would be taken from the parents or close relatives to the effect that the children were given with their own approval and that they no longer were connected to their families. The jariyes were priced according to their beauty, the regularity of their bodies and their age. Just as sick ones were returned to their owners or families, those with heavy sleep who snored or who had any other defect would usually not be purchased. If a girl had a missing tooth, the price would be lowered. If she was flatfooted, it was considered to be unlucky; either she would not be bought or she would be sold with difficulty.

When the accounts of the sultan's private budget were examined, it was seen that the palace could purchase jariyes when needed. During the reign of Sultan Abdülmecid a jariye would be purchased by the palace for 60,000 kuruş; in Sultan Abdülaziz's reign a Circassian jariye was purchased for 20,000 kuruş.

There were sometimes clowns, black women, dwarfs and dumb girls among the jariyes bought. When the receipts of the jariyes bought for the palace were examined, it was found that some elderly women, wet

Jules Joseph Lefebvre, *Servant*, 1880, detail, oil on canvas, 128 x 82.5 cm, (İmparatorluktan Portreler, p. 139).

nurses and educated women who would be governesses were present. The eunuchs from the palace handled this task; in fact, they made a profession out of the white jariye trade. In addition, state officials also played a role in procuring jariyes for the palace.

Novice jariyes were taught palace customs by the treasury usta and kalfas. First they were taken to the Novice Corps; then they were trained by the palace's prominent ustas and their assistants. Novice jariyes were given in groups of 5-7 to the command of a scribe kalfa, who would give lessons for three years with an emphasis on subjects that would enhance their refinement and taste like music, dance, harmony of carriage, manner, palace style, customs and handiwork, rather than reading and writing.

They were also taught things like what kind of attitude of respect was to be taken while offering a beverage or slippers and underwear to a sultan or prince or while their master was washing his hands. Those with talent were also taught to play the piano, paint and speak foreign languages. During the training period of the novices they would never take permanent duty in any chamber.

All novice jariyes were raised according to Islamic rules. Just as pages left the inner court, girls in the harem would leave the palace when their periods of duty were over by being married to a high-ranking soldier or bureaucrat. In these conditions, the harem can also be seen as a school for training slave wives for the sultan and his favorite male slaves. According to the observations of Postel on the mid-16th century Imperial Harem, the sultan had the jariyes in the harem educated like his own daughters.

Osman Hamdi, *A Young Girl Having Her Hair Combed*, detail, oil on canvas, 39 x 58 cm, National Palaces Collection.

Kalfas looked after these novice jariyes just like a mother and they were fully responsible for the girls. When an assistant stewardess announced that a novice jariye had been trained, the treasury stewardess or sometimes even the sultan's mother would examine the girl as if she were in a test. The jariyes would be recompensed and rewarded according to their loyalty and service to their masters.

After the novices completed their basic and preparatory training periods, they would enter service alongside a kalfa. Just as novices served in the chambers of wives and princesses or princes, they could also serve in the sultan's chambers. Those outstanding with their capabilities, physical aspects and behavior would be specially trained by the treasury kalfas and they would be under the protection of the sultan's mother. Overseeing the quarters of the jariyes, the distribution of their salaries and the protection of their doors were the responsibility of the Aghas of the House of Serenity.

Just as this type of jariye was presented for service in the sultan's chambers, the sultan could also choose them as mates. However, just as every novice page in the Inner Courtyard could not directly serve the sultan and become a state official, every jariye in the palace could not enter the sultan's chambers and give service in these chambers.

The others besides those who stood out in the harem with various special characteristics and had good fortune were utilized in the ordinary work of the harem. Black jariyes, in particular, were employed in slightly heavier tasks; jobs like cleaning the floors, corridors and walls were performed by black jariyes. Cleaning water pipes, cleaning and mending sofa cushions, helping to prepare sherbet and rice, etc. were considered to be light work.

The refined and disciplined training given made the harem into a nest of culture and courtesy. In the memoirs of those who lived in the harem it is related that experienced jariyes told novices, "Someone who does not attain good manners in the palace cannot learn etiquette anywhere; this is a finishing school."

When Safiye Ünüvar, a teacher during the reign of Sultan Mehmed (Reşad) V, first came to the palace, the Circassian jariyes mentioned palace courtesy and grooming with pride. Ünüvar related that after that moment she better understood why generals and gentlemen preferred to marry palace women.

2. Kalfas (Assistant Stewardesses)

The rank of kalfa was second in the jariye hierarchy. After novice jariyes were trained, they rose in the ranks and became kalfas. They were distributed among the chambers of the sultan, the valide sultan, princes and wives according to their physical characteristics and capabilities. The most important services in the harem were provided directly by the kalfas. While the kalfas served the chambers, they also trained the novices. The chamber's highest ranking kalfa was called the chief kalfa or senior jariye. Middle and low-ranking kalfas came after the chief kalfa. The chief kalfa or senior kalfa was responsible for the chamber's order and all tasks. Princesses and princes showed respect to the chief kalfa and addressed her as "kafam."

The jariyes and kalfas serving in the palace were called "saraylı" (from the palace) by those outside the palace. In return, those living in the palace called non-members of the palace who lived in the city "şehirli" (from the city). It is related that the "saraylı" used the term "şehirli" as an expression of lower status.

The kalfas gave every kind of service to the chamber where they were on duty. The owner of the chamber would choose the chief kalfa from among those jariyes given to the chamber. In the selection of chief kalfa seniority was not the main criterion; characteristics like intelligence, loyalty and capability were more important. Consequently, the owner of the chamber would choose one of the kalfas with these characteristics. Towards the end of the 19th century the senior jariye or chief kalfa was also called the directress of the chamber.

Senior kalfas did not do heavy work. There were middle and low-ranking kalfas under her command. The middle kalfa served the master of the chamber. The low-ranking kalfas served the middle and great kalfas. The kalfas were on duty one week in the chamber alongside the jariyes who were with them. They would clean the whole chamber on Thursday. This was called the Thursday service.

On Friday they would turn over their duties to the other kalfas and then would rest until their turn came again. Together with the other jariyes, the kalfa in each chamber would bring in the food brought by the food carriers; then they would distribute it to the tray tables that had been set up. The novice jariyes would clean the tray tables and wash the dishes. Personal service to the wives like putting her bedroom in order, combing her hair and dressing her were the responsibility of the kalfas.

Another of the duties of the senior kalfas was to greet guests. Taking the veils and outer garments of the guests coming to the palace, ironing them and putting them into bundles and giving them back to their owners were among some other duties of the senior kalfa. When a wife's chamber was visited, first the guest would meet with the senior kalfa, drink coffee and then be taken by the senior kalfa to the wife's room on the upper floor. As can be understood here, it was not compatible with palace custom to go directly to see the wife.

Fifteen-twenty kalfas in the staff of the palace's most experienced jariyes would be on guard every night; they would sit in the sultan's anteroom in the harem from the night prayer until morning and walk around the gardens of all the chambers two or three at a time. These were called guardian kalfas. If there were an accident or illness at night, they would immediately inform the head scribe. In order not to sleep, they would eat a night meal, and while some walked around the grounds, others played games. A general house cleaning was made at the beginning of every month. Middle kalfas together with the young girls cleaned all the anterooms, the corridors, the steps, the baths and basement floor. They would sprinkle soap bubbles on everything including the thin Egyptian mats spread on the floors and then clean them.

Other than the tasks in the chambers, the kalfas also had duties in the general services of the harem. The harem's dancers and musicians were among the kalfas. Also these women played a top role in the training of jariyes in every area. Almost all the senior kalfas could read and write.

3. Ustas (Stewardesses)

The highest rank jariyes on duty in the harem institution could reach was the rank of usta. Jariyes outstanding among their peers with various special characteristics could attain this position. Just as there were ustas serving the sultan, the valide sultan also had ustas. Ustas also performed duty in the chambers of the princesses who had left the palaces and the princes. However, there being no ustas in the chambers of the wives and favorites of the sultan shows that the employment of jariyes with this rank was unique to harem members with blood ties to the dynasty.

Regardless of which chamber they were in, the number and title of the ustas did not change. These were: the treasury usta, the laundry usta, the lady butler, the usta of the sultan's ewer, the coffee usta , the usta of headdresses, and the usta of the pantry. In addition to these main ustas, there were also ustas in the general service of the harem like the deputy usta , the medical usta, the stokers usta , and the palace usta. The treasury usta was the most influential among the stewardesses. In the position as chief of all the jariyes in the Imperial Harem, she was the most influential person in the harem after the valide sultan, the wives, the princes and princesses. Just as the valide sultan was at the head of the harem, the treasury usta was the chief of the jariyes. The treasury usta performed her duty with the help of the assistant treasury ustas and the novices.

The main duty of the treasury stewardesses was private service to the sultan. When the sultan was in the harem, he saw the treasury usta most and would communicate his decisions by means of her. And again, as long as the sultan was in the harem, she would not leave the Sultan's Chamber. The treasury stewardess could go and sit next to the sultan. The second and third treasury ustas could always enter the sultan's presence and perform their services. The wife or favorite to be invited by the sultan was invited by means of the treasury usta. Third, fourth and fifth treasurers, together with the kalfas they took with them stood guard in front of the sultan's chamber day and night. The treasury usta carried the keys to all the treasuries in the harem.

If princesses or even wives wanted something, they would have the treasury usta informed or if something was needed by the palace, she would be informed. Her chamber would be furnished according to her position, and she had many jariyes in her service. Her salary and provisions were high. She would manage the harem chamber with the treasurers in her retinue. The ceremonial process related to the hosting of the wives or daughters of foreign heads of state or the wives of foreign ambassadors also was administered by the treasury usta.

Number 88 Second Mounting Hall, Entrance to the Sultan's Chamber in the Harem. There are rooms around this hall belonging to the treasury usta and her kalfas.

The middle and lower floors of the sultan's chamber in the Dolmabahçe Palace Harem were assigned to the treasury usta and the other treasury kalfas on her staff and the novices. While the treasury usta and the second treasury usta used the rooms on the middle floor, the other treasurers were settled in the rooms on the ground floor. The novices under the command of the treasury kalfas stayed in the dormitories in the basement floor. In periods when the valide sultan was not alive, her chamber would be assigned to the treasury usta, not the head wife. The tradition of placing the treasury usta close to the valide sultan can be seen in the Topkapı Palace as well.

Because the treasury usta was in the position of spokeswoman of the sultan in the harem, the sultan would relate his oral commands to the women of the palace by means of her and while the treasury usta announced the sultan's decrees, it was palace custom to stand up. If it is necessary to make a comparison, the keys of the treasuries and depots in the harem were with the treasury usta. Whatever the position of the marshal of the sultan's household or the head chamberlain was in the official section of the palace (Imperial Mabeyn), the treasury usta was in the same position in the harem.

The treasury kalfas were the highest ranking of all the kalfas in the harem and their number ranged from 15-20. They stood guard day and night in groups of four. The first three of the treasury kalfas could enter the presence of the sultan to perform service to him; the others could only do so when called to do so.

The sultan's female servants -most of whom were senior and junior kalfas given to harem chambers- were divided into groups and performed a 24-hour guard duty per week together with the sultan's head guards in the anteroom below the sultan's anteroom. On the other days, according to their rank, the female servants of the sultan and those of young age together with the middle-ranked kalfas in the chamber they were in, would perform one week of coffee service to the sultan, serve one week food-taster, one week in the kitchen and two days as room guard. They would clean the whole chamber on Thursday and turn over duty to the other guards on Friday.

No one had the authority to approach the chamber where the sultan lived without invitation, especially his bedroom. Only the treasury usta and kalfas on guard could enter every chamber when necessary. Jariyes serving the wives and favorite concubines could not enter the sultan's chamber.

From the National Palaces' Collection:

1 Tea Set

2 Coffee Set

During the reign of Abdülhamid II, the treasury usta would perform duty as hostess and she would host the wives of statesmen who were guests at the palace in the Ceremonial Hall in the Yıldız Palace, which was used as the Imperial Guesthouse. When these women came to the palace, they would kiss the skirt of the treasury usta.

The sultan would choose the treasury ustas from the kalfas whom he trusted and was familiar with; for this reason, when the sultan changed, so would the treasury usta and treasury kalfas. Just as in the classical period when pages who performed the private services of the sultan and who served in his chamber rose in the ranks in the inner courtyard, the treasury usta and kalfas were chosen from among the most distinguished and talented jariyes in the harem.

Şadiye Sultan, one of the daughters of Abdülhamid II, wrote in her memoirs regarding the treasury usta:

"The treasury usta carried a wand made from ivory embellished with diamonds, emeralds and rubies. The first three assistant stewardesses carried the same wand, but the diamonds were smaller and the ornamentation was simpler. The dresses of the usta and kalfas were made from pink and white brocade. The edges were trimmed with broad silver or gold thread, and they wore a loose jacket called a salta. The small embellished hat on her head called a hotuz, the richness of her jewels, broche and pins, the graveness and seriousness of her actions and the attitudes of respect and modesty of those around her enabled the treasury usta to be easily spotted."

In addition to the treasury usta's being the top administrator in the harem, she also represented the valide sultan in protocol. For example, the treasury usta welcomed the mother of the Egyptian Khedive, who was known as Pasha Mother, at the Yıldız Chalet.

Usually the kalfas serving the meals were called çaşnigir or çeşniyar (lady butler). A çaşnigir stewardess would be found at the head of this group. There were kalfas and jariyes on her staff. Their duty was to protect the food and dishes belonging to the sultan.

This name was also given to the head of those washing the sultan's clothing. The kalfa of highest rank in her staff was the second çaşnigir. There were also other kalfas on her staff. The Dolmabahçe Palace laundry was located on the lower floor of the sultan's chamber in the harem. The harem laundry was washed in stone tubs.

The head of the jariyes who helped the sultan wash his hands and face and make ablution was called the ewer usta and her assistant was the second ewer usta. She had sufficient kalfas on her staff. In addition, the ewer stewardess protected the basin, ewer and towels belonging to the sultan.

The barber usta headed the kalfas who took care of the sultan's shaving set. Her assistant was called the second barber usta. She also had kalfas with her.

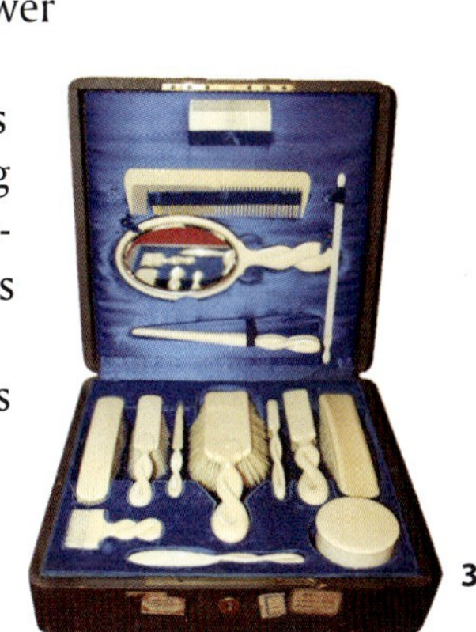

The coffee usta headed the kalfas who brewed the sultan's coffee and protected his coffee sets. Her assistant was the second coffee usta, and there were also kalfas who helped

From the National Palaces' Collection:

1 Enema Set

2 Towel

3 Toilette Set

4 Grooming Set belonging to Sultan Abdülhamid II

with this service. Important work befell the coffee stewardess and her assistants during ceremonies, especially during religious holidays. Among their main duties was the preparation and dispensing of coffee to the women and princesses who came to give their congratulations on the holidays. They performed these duties quickly and masterfully.

The head of the kalfas who took care of the sultan's pantry and pantry sets was called the pantry usta. Her assistant was the second pantry usta. She performed her duty with jariyes given to her command. Sherbets, fruit and snacks belonging to the sultan were kept in his pantry. Together with the çaşnigar usta, the pantry usta served the sultan while he was eating. When it was necessary to serve the sultan sherbet and fruit, this duty was performed by the pantry usta together with her assistant jariyes.

The mistress of headdresses and her assistants helped the princesses, wives and favorite concubines to bathe, dress and in their grooming. Later on princesses and wives had their own personal head-dressers.

In the first half of the 20th century stewardesses on duty in the Imperial Harem no longer performed the indicated tasks; only their ranks remained. They had their own retinues and personal harem aghas. However, all of these trained the young girls in the palace in addition to the special duties mentioned.

4. Other Jariyes with Authority

In addition to those mentioned above, there were other jariyes who performed administrative and support service. Their main titles were as follows:

Deputy Usta

At the head of all the jariyes in the harem, the treasury usta would appoint a deputy to manage, in her name, all the jariyes living in the jariye quarters. She was called the deputy stewardess. Her chamber was in the chamber of the jariyes. She was always at their head, she would give the necessary commands and she helped in their training.

Harem Stewardesses

The harem usta was the harem's hostes. By the time of the second decade in the 17th century, she had taken her place among the prominent administrators in the harem. This stemmed in part from her high rank as the most senior administrator in the institution of the harem and from her role in training women for personal service to the sultan. She would oversee all harem ceremonies for weddings, births and holiday celebrations and teach the jariyes what kind of relationship to have with the sultan and all members of the dynasty and how to act. One of her names was "Palace Stewardess."

Head Clerk

The supervisors who enforced the harem's discipline, ceremonies and order were called the head scribe, second scribe, third scribe and fourth scribe. The head scribe followed the treasury usta in regard to the harem ceremonial ranking. In addition, she had kalfas to assist her. Scribe kalfas were chosen from experienced, alert and capable jariyes. They would assist the harem usta kalfas were also chosen from veteran servants and were experienced servants to the sultan.

From among the administrative jariyes, the head scribe kalfa handled correspondence between the sultan and princesses inside and outside the palace and with other harem officials and correspondence with the Mabeyn and the Ministry of the Imperial Treasury related to the salaries, residence records, cancellation of records, deaths, appointments, etc.

Daye (Wet-nurse) and Dada (Governess) Kalfas

The jariyes employed or bought to nurse the sultan's daughters and princes were called daye, taye or sütnine. It is known that there were wet-nurses from the early days of the Ottomans. Because the wet-nurses would breast-feed future sultans, it was necessary that they be the wives of good people and members of good families. Wet-nurses with jariye roots were generally from the rank of kalfa. During the classical period the relationship between the sultan and wet-nurse was seen as a mother and child relationship. When the sultan's mother died before him, his wet-nurse would take on a role of guidance. Ümmü Gülsüm Hatun, the wet-nurse of Mehmed II, was granted enough income from the sultan to have two mosques constructed in İstanbul and one mosque in Edirne.

There were wet-nurses in the 19th century palace as well. It was determined from salary records that there was a wet-nurse in each wife's chamber. The wet-nurse was ranked third hierarchically after the head kalfa and the governess kalfa. It is also understood from the records that when wet-nurse kalfas were acquired by the palace to nurse the princes or princesses, they brought their

Ayşe Osmanoğlu, a daughter of Sultan Abdülhamid II.

children with them. Recorded as the "daughter of the wet-nurse," these children were also given daily stipends. It is known that the wet-nurses had great influence in the palace until the end of the sultanate.

The jariyes and women who took care of the sultan's children and served them personally were called dadı (governess). Ayşe Sultan, the daughter of Sultan Abdülhamid II, describes her governess as follows:

"I was very familiar with her. When I was young, she would put me to bed and sit at the head of the bed. She would sing lullabies in a delicate voice until I fell asleep. During the day she told me beautiful stories; she would dress me with infinite care, compassion, affection and she did everything for me. I would kiss her on the cheek and say, "My dear Dada," and she would say "My only one, my angel sultan."

A child of the sultan would not be given to anyone other than the wet-nurse and governess to hold. When the child began to walk, its governess would follow him/her, and there would be small jariyes around to entertain him/her with toys. The children would go out with their wet-nurses and governesses.

Master of Patients and Usta

The chief medical officer was responsible for following up the care and treatment of jariyes in the harem who were ill. She was followed by the medical usta and the other kalfas. It was found in a study that during the reign of Sultan Abdülmecid this staff included 17 jariyes (the chief medical jariye and medical usta included). It can be understood that the chief medical officer was in a higher hierarchic rank when their place in the salary records is examined and when it is seen that she received 500 kuruş more than the medical usta.

Chief Stoker and Usta

The jariyes who stoked the fires for the baths were called "stoker jariyes" and the chief jariye was called the bath (stoker) usta. According to a record of salaries during the reign of Sultan Abdülmecid, there were approximately 10 stoker jariyes. While the salary of the stewardess of the bath was 200 kuruş, the salaries of the others ranged from 100-125 according to rank. They also received a yearly bonus called a muharremiye.

The stoker usta handled the cleaning of all the silver and brass braziers used by members of the harem, the care and needs of the baths and stoke holes, and the acquisition of wood and coal. The same tasks under the responsibility of the chief stoker in the Imperial Mabeyn belonged to the bath usta in the harem.

5. The Staff of Kalfas in the Chambers

The general protocol and hierarchical order of behavior in the Ottoman palace was felt by the service staff in the harem chambers as well. For example, this was seen between the senior kalfas, their assistants and the kalfas and the novices. General dining trays were set up for the jariyes in the chamber with the exception of the senior kalfa; she had her own private dining tray. The novice jariyes would set up these trays. If she liked, the senior kalfa could eat together with other kalfas of her own rank. Even if their dining trays were not as elaborate as their master's, still they were well adorned. The girls in service took care of these one week at a time; another group would take over service during the next week. There were also middle and junior ranked kalfas in the chambers in addition to the senior kalfas. They worked under the supervision of the senior kalfas. The middle and junior ranked kalfas trained the novice jariyes who were new at the palace. The novice jariyes called the junior ranked kalfas who were in the position of their first teachers, "küçüfam" (my junior kalfa). The new jariyes performed the same service and showed the same obedience to their senior and junior kalfas as they did to their masters. They were trained in religion and reading and writing.

There was a certain distance between the kalfas and the wives of the sultan to whom these chambers belonged. The kalfas sat on cushions before the wives rather than on couches; this can be shown as an example of the hierarchical relationship between them.

The wives would invite the senior kalfas to share a meal. The duties of the kalfas in the chamber, particularly the senior kalfa, included being at the side of the wife, conversing with her, informing her of important information, and being present at her side during ceremonies and festivities.

6. The Tragic Situation of Jariyes in Changes in the Throne

As long as the sultan was on the throne, the Imperial Harem was comfortable, but in cases of the death of the sultan or his dethronement, members of the harem received their share of difficult times. In the early years of the empire, wives of the sultan would accompany their sons to the provincial districts and pass their lives there. Later when the sultan died, his mother, wives, favorites and even jariyes he liked very much and the treasury usta and kalfas in close service to them would lose all their privileges and be taken from their chambers to the Old Palace. Housing the women of former sultans until the year 1826, the Old Palace was called the "Palace of Tears" for this reason. This palace was located in the place where the İstanbul University rectory is located today. This structure was given to the Ministry of War in 1826, and the women here were transferred to the Topkapı Palace and the Çifte Palaces.

However, when the system of seniority changed during the reign of Ahmed I, the harem withdrew to within four walls. Until the middle of the 18th century, in situations like this they passed their lives in the Old Palace sequestered from the outside world.

This situation changed towards the end of the 18th century. Beginning with this period both wives of the sultan and wealthy former wives of the sultan could live outside the palace in mansions. The Feriye Palaces constructed in Ortaköy during the Reform Period were set aside as residences for members of the families of former sultans. In other words, during the Reform Period, the Feriye Palaces were designated as official residences of the wives, consorts, princes and princesses of former sultans. In addition, it is known that towards the end of the sultanate some of the wives of sultans who had died resided at private shore houses.

In the case of dethronement this situation was even more tragic. After Sultan Abdülaziz was dethroned by means of a coup d'état, hundreds of jariyes were sent out of the palace and their jewels were plundered; moreover, the wives of the dethroned sultan and even his mother were subject to more severe treatment. A similar situation occurred with the dethronement of Abdülhamid II: Some of the jariyes turned out from the Yıldız Palace were married and some were returned to their families. Close to fifty jariyes who had no relatives suffered financial difficulties for months; eventually with a governmental decision a salary was given to them. Jariyes who had been clothed and trained by their masters in the Imperial Harem had to eventually run after a place of refuge and food to eat.

Pierre Desire Guillemet, *Black Servant*, 1873, 100 x 82 cm, oil on canvas, Sabancı Museum Collection, (Osmanlı Sarayı'nda Oryantalistler, p. 25).

The Structure, Architecture and Layout of the Imperial Harem in the 19th Century

The traditional layout of the Topkapı Palace was continued in the harem section of the palaces built in the 19th century, and both the jariye and wives' sections were arranged at a distance from the sultan's private chamber. The chamber of the valide sultan was in a dominant position and the harem was planned around her chambers in the main palaces of the period like the Dolmabahçe Palace, the Beylerbeyi Palace and the Çırağan Palace.

There is no chamber under the name Jariyes' Chamber in the Harem which is located in the Dolmabahçe, for this is not possible according to the harem protocol. Jariyes were only found in the harem for service and their master's chamber was not a permanent residence for them, rather it was a place of duty they used during their service. The real residence of jariyes of different ranks (usta, kalfa, etc.) on duty in various chambers in the palace was constructed separate from the harem, but close to it and was called the New Chamber. Today the technical units tied to the National Palaces use this building.

The novice, kalfa and usta jariyes on the staff of the harem chambers used these chambers, especially the ground and middle floors, during their terms of service. When the layout of the chambers in the harem is examined, the dominant position of the Valide Sultan (Sultan's Mother) Chamber is striking. The Valide Sultan Chamber and the Sultan's Chamber were designed next to one another

Dolmabahçe Palace, Harem Section (Imperial Harem).

with a view of the sea. The chambers of the wives are after the Valide Sultan Chamber. Consequently, it is impossible to pass to the Sultan's Chamber without being seen from the Valide Sultan Chamber. The chambers of the wives are visually plainer both in their position and architecture than the Valide Sultan Chamber. The most magnificent of the chambers in the Dolmabahçe Palace Harem is the Sultan's Chamber. If the harem is compared to a pyramid, the valide sultan is at its summit and the novices are the lowest. The jariyes not only comprised the service staff of the palace, but beyond this, the mother, wives and favorite consorts of the sultan were mostly chosen from jariyes. In other words, the institution of the jariyes was very important for the harem; a correct understanding of the harem can only be possible with an approach that considers this institution with its different aspects and with an objective approach.

When the harem divisions, layout plan, architectural elements, protocol, etc. of the

The Jariyes' Chambers in the Dolmabahçe Palace (used today as the Directorate of Restoration and Infrastructure).

Ottoman palaces are examined, it can be understood what kind of function the Imperial Harem possessed. The ideal expression of 19th century palace organization and harem life can be found in the Dolmabahçe Palace. Whether in the Dolmabahçe Palace or the other palaces of the time like the Beylerbeyi and Çırağan palaces, the harem layout is the same. The order of the chambers in the harem is the Sultan's Chamber, the Valide Sultan Chamber and the chambers of the wives. The traditional layout plan of the Topkapı Palace was continued. Both the jariye section and the wives' section were arranged at a distance from the sultan's private chamber. It is seen that the Valide Sultan Chamber is dominant in the main palaces of the period like the Dolmabahçe Palace, the Beylerbeyi Palace and the Çırağan Palace.

The harem section of the Dolmabahçe Palace is comprised of spaces arranged for the sultan, valide sultan, the wives of the sultan, the princes and princesses. In this section of

Dolmabahçe Palace, Harem Section (Imperial Harem).

the palace there are a total of 10 chambers, 8 of which were for the sultan's wives and favorite concubines. The princes and princesses lived in the chambers of their mothers (or god-mothers if their mothers were not living.)

The first two chambers constructed parallel to the sea in the harem section of the Dolmabahçe Palace are the chambers of the sultan and valide sultan. The chambers of the wives follow these and were constructed perpendicular to the sea. In other words, the only section of the palace that has no visual tie with the outer world is the chambers of the wives. All the chambers in the harem were arranged as 3 stories; in addition, an attic floor was allocated for each chamber.

The Sultan's Chamber in the Harem

The Sultan's Chamber is the first of the two chambers in the harem parallel to the sea and it is the most magnificent. Like the other chambers in the harem, this chamber has three floors and an attic floor. While the top floor of the chamber was the sultan's living space, the middle and ground floors were used by the jariyes in the service class.

The Sultan's Chamber is the most magnificent of the chambers in the harem, for the Ottoman sultan who filled both the office of the sultanate and the office of the caliphate lived in this chamber. Consequently, in addition to this chamber being the sultan's residence, it also symbolized the sultanate and the caliphate.

It was not a palace custom for the sultan's wives and favorite concubines, princes and princesses to enter the Sultan's Chamber uninvited; there were certain rules and discipline for entering this chamber. In particular, no one had the authority to approach the place where the sultan sat and his bedroom. Only the treasury usta and the kalfas on guard duty entered every chamber when necessary. They acted with great silence. The treasury jariyes wore thin slippers without heels made from soft leather or fabric. These slippers were special to the Sultan's Chamber. They wore other shoes outside the Sultan's Chamber. No sound louder than the sultan's voice could be heard in this chamber. When it was necessary for a wife, favorite concubine or princess from the Imperial Harem to come to the sultan's chamber, she would be invited by one of the treasury kalfas on duty in the sultan's chambers.

The Sultan's Chamber in the Dolmabahçe Harem is a very spacious and richly furnished

Dolmabahçe Palace, Blue Hall in the Sultan's Chamber in the Imperial Harem.

1

2

3

4

5

space with a view of the sea. Here there were two bedrooms belonging to the sultan. The first of these is the summer bedroom on the land-side and the other is the winter bedroom on the sea-side. The other rooms in the Sultan's Chamber were: a Writing Room, a Clothing Room, a Bath, a Guestroom, a Treasury Room (Taş Oda) and a Coffee Hearth. Because these chambers belonged not only to the Ottoman ruler, but to the caliph of all Muslims, there were also a Sakal-ı Şerif Room (where hairs from the beard of the Prophet Muhammad were kept) and a Guard Room where treasury kalfas on duty in this chamber stayed.

1 Red Room, the Sultan's Private Room.

2 Room Number 69 in the Sultan's Chamber in the Dolmabahçe Harem, Writing Chamber/ Atatürk's Study. Because it was used by the treasury kalfas for the purpose of keeping watch, it was also called the Guard Room.

3 Room Number 63 in the Sultan's Chamber in the Dolmabahçe Harem, the Sakal-ı Şerif Room.

4 The Clothing Room in the Sultan's Chamber. All clothing, swords, accessories and jewels belonging to the sultan were kept in this room.

5 The Sultan's Bath (Ceramic Tile Bath).

The Valide Sultan's Chamber

In line with tradition, the chamber after the Sultan's Chamber in the harem section of the Dolmabahçe Palace was the Valide Sultan's Chamber. Like the Sultan's Chamber, these chambers also had a view of the sea. The chamber has three main floors and an attic floor. The service stairs and various functional doors and corridors indicate the actively functional state of the Valide Sultan's Chamber.

The Valide Sultan's Chamber being located between the Sultan's Chamber and the chambers of the wives is compatible with the valide sultan's monitoring position in the harem hierarchy. Due to this layout plan, it is possible for the valide sultan to follow passages from the Wives' Chambers to the Sultan's Chamber. In regard to design of the space and its location, there are aspects of the Valide Sultan Chamber that distinguish it from the chambers of the wives: The Wives Chambers have the appearance of "lined up chambers"

Daytime Sitting Room number 110, Valide Sultan Chamber.

Number 114, Valide Sultan Bedroom.

and they all resemble one another, whereas, the Valide Sultan Chamber has a view of the sea on one side and its design arrangement is different. This architectural arrangement shows the superiority of the valide sultan in the harem.

On the top floor of the Valide Sultan Chamber there are such spaces as the Audience Hall (Pink Hall), the Daytime Sitting Room, Bedroom, Guest Bedroom, Turkish Bath, Scribes Chamber, Adile Sultan Chamber and Sultan's Room. It can be understood from examined archive records that Sultan Abdülaziz had his own room in his mother's chamber and that he visited his mother Pertevniyal Valide Sultan at regular intervals as her guest. However, there is no record of a room belonging to the sultan in chambers of the wives or favorite consorts. There being rooms designated for the sultan and his sister Adile Sultan in the Valide Sultan Chamber can be considered an architectural statement of the Valide Sultan Chamber being a focal point of power of shared sultanate authority.

Together with there being some spaces used by the valide sultan on the middle floor, this floor and the ground floor were designated for the stewardess and kalfas. According to the records of salaries during the reigns of Sultan Abdülmecid and Sultan Abdülaziz, there were approximately 100-150 jariyes (ustas, kalfas and novices) in the Valide Sultan Chamber.

1 Number 115, Valide Sultan Private Room, Valide Sultan Chamber.

2 Door opening to number 112 anteroom and service stairway in the Valide Sultan Chamber. The door on two sides of the service stairways opens to the corridor where the Wives Chambers were located.

1

2

Wives Chambers

Number 179, Wives' Chamber

3 Number 181, Sitting Room.

4 Number 180, Bedroom.

5 Number 182, Sitting Room.

One of the three main chambers in the Imperial Harem section of the Dolmabahçe Palace belongs to the wives; favorite consorts also used this chamber. While the first two chambers (the Sultan's Chamber and the Valide Sultan Chamber) have views of the sea,

3

4

5

the chamber of the wives was designed perpendicular to the sea, thus assuring privacy.

The chambers where the sultan's wives and children lived were arranged on three floors plus an attic floor. The top floor included a bedroom for its mistress, a daytime sitting room, a bedroom for the prince or princess, and a room for the head kalfa. On the middle floor there was a bedroom, a dining room, and a room for the kalfas. On the ground floor there was a room for dishwashing, a pantry, a laundry and places where the novices lived; there was also a toilet and hand basin on each floor and a service stairway between the floors. In addition, there were storage cupboards where objects that were used at night like mattresses and sheets were stored during the day. The attic which was reached by the service stairway from the top floor was used for kalfas and novices to stay in and included various service units. Also it has been determined that there was a birthing room in the chambers of the wives and favorite concubines.

1

Decorative objects:
1 Detail from colored glass chandelier with bunch of grapes, Number 182 Sitting Room.

Just as in the other rooms and halls in the palace, there were door curtains on all the doors in the Wives' Chambers. The spaces were adorned with cushions for special guests and others, thin mattresses to sit on, pillows and stairway cushions and consoles with mirrors. Heat was provided by silver and brass braziers and linoleum was placed

2

3

2 Number 158, Wife's Chamber, detail from one of cornices with scenery in the center.
3 Room number 169, detail from cornices with flower motif.

under them to prevent fires. Different qualities of mats like Egyptian, Indian and Tunisian mats were spread on the floors and rugs from Uşak and Manisa-Gördes were laid on top of those. The richness of the rooms was accentuated with curtains made from Hereke brocade and silk material, furbelows, fringe, tassels and gilded cornices.

The service staff for the Wives' Chamber was comprised of jariyes (kalfas and novices), harem aghas and halberdiers in accordance with the structure of the harem. Between 5 and 10 kalfas would be on duty in each chamber; their head was called the head jariye, head kalfa or senior kalfa. The governess headed the jariye staff who served the princes and princesses, and she was followed by the wet nurse. The external ties of the wives were handled by the harem aghas;

1

Decorative objects:

1 Number 158, Wife's Chamber, Far Eastern crafted closet**.**

2 Number 172, Wife's Chamber, detail of bird figure from Japanese folding screen.

however, they did not enter the chambers of the women, but at most they could stand at the entrance of the anterooms in the chambers. The harem agha was called "agha." The halberdiers handled the coffee, carriage and porter services of the sultan's wives and they stayed in the Halberdier Chamber, the facade of which was on Dolmabahçe Avenue.

2

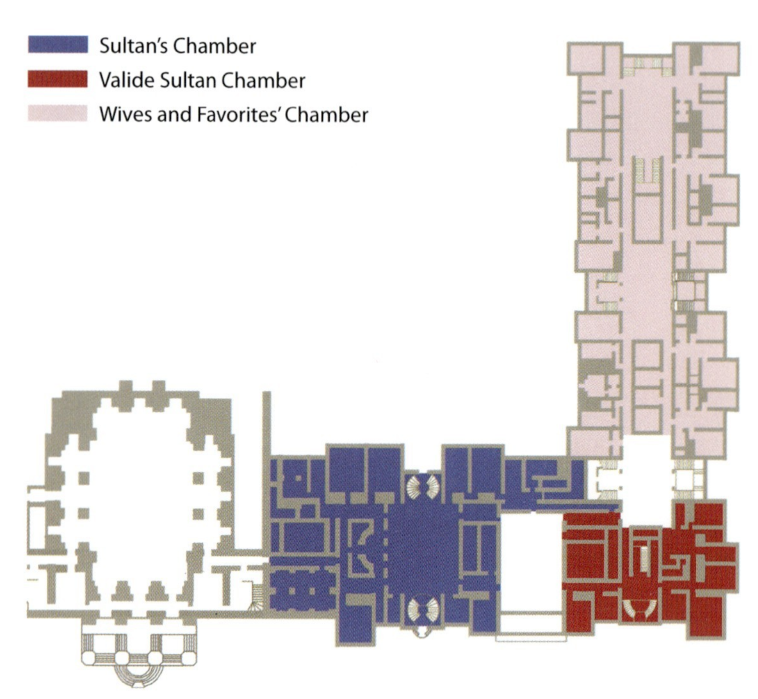

Dolmabahçe Palace Imperial Harem, ground floor.

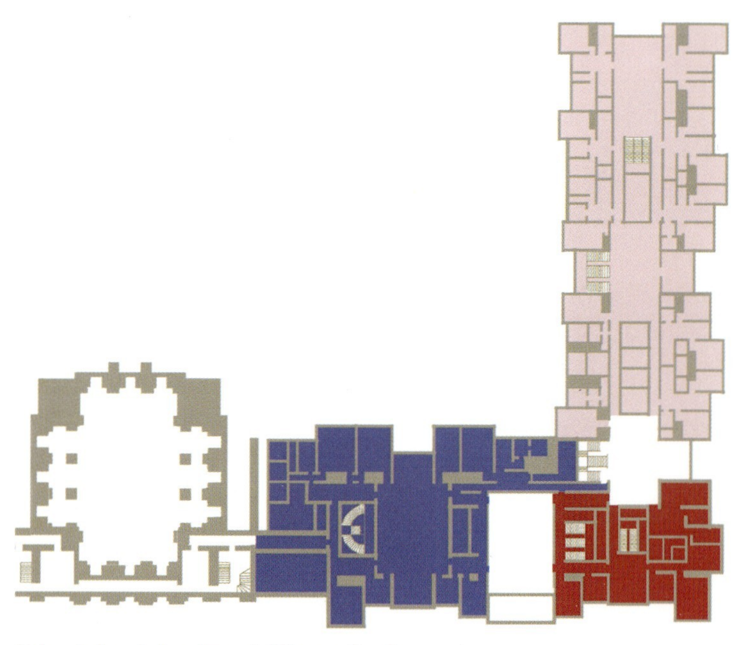

Dolmabahçe Palace Imperial Harem, first floor.

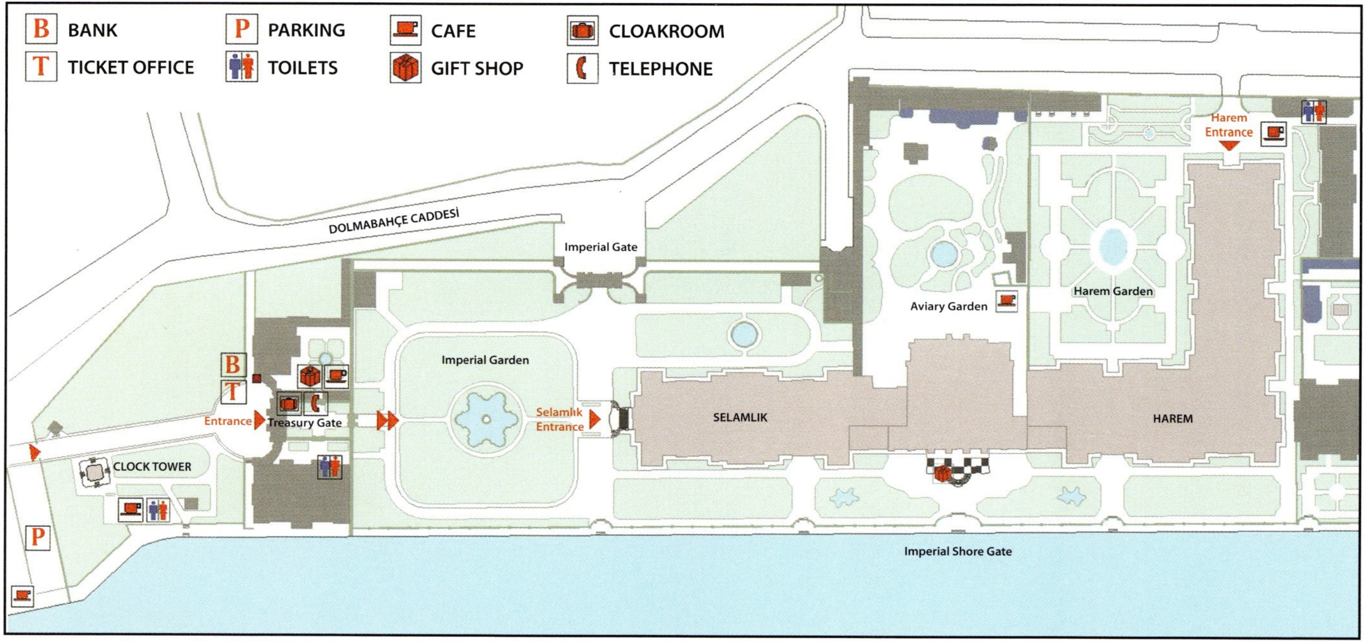

BANK
TICKET OFFICE
PARKING
TOILETS
CAFE
GIFT SHOP
CLOAKROOM
TELEPHONE

DOLMABAHÇE CADDESİ
Imperial Gate
Harem Entrance
Aviary Garden
Harem Garden
Imperial Garden
Entrance
Treasury Gate
Selamlık Entrance
SELAMLIK
HAREM
CLOCK TOWER
Imperial Shore Gate

Dolmabahçe Palace layout plan.

BIBLIOGRAPHY

I- ARCHIVE REFERENCES

A. Prime Ministry Ottoman Archive

a- Documents

1. Bâb-ı Âli Evrak Odası Sadâret Evrakı
   - Bâb-ı Âli Evrak Odası (BEO)
   - Sadâret Divân Kalemî (A.DVN).
   - Mektûbî Kalemî, Meclis-i Vâlâ (A.MKT.MVL).
   - Mektûbî Kalemî, Umum Vilâyât (A.MKT.UM).
   - Sadâret Mektûbî Kalemî (A.MKT).
   - Mektûbî Kalemî, Nezâret ve Devair (A.MKT.NZD).

2. Cevdet Tasnifi
   - Cevdet, Saray Mesalihi (C.SM).

3. Dâhiliye Nezâreti Evrakı
   - Dâhiliye Nezâreti, Kalem-i Mahsûs Evrakı (DH.KMS).

4. Hazine-i Hassa Evrakı (Dosya Envanter Tasnifi-DES)
   - Hazine-i Hassa, İradeler (HH.İ).
   - Hazine-i Hassa, Mefruşat Ambarı (HH.MFŞ).
   - Hazine-i Hassa, Muhasebe (HH.MH).

5. İrade Tasnifi
   - İrade, Hususî (İ.HUS).
   - İrade, Mesail-i Mühime (İ.MSM).

6. Mâbeyn-i Hümâyûn Evrakı (DES)
   - Mâbeyn-i Hümâyûn (MB).
   - Mâbeyn-i Hümâyûn, İradeler (MB.İ).

7. Meclis-i Vâlâ Evrakı
   - Meclis-i Vâlâ Evrakı (MVL).

8. Meclis-i Vükela Mazbataları
   - Meclis-i Vükela Mazbataları (MV).

9. Yıldız Tasnifi
   - Yıldız Perakende Evrakı, Arzuhal ve Jurnaller (Y.PRK.AZJ).
   - Yıldız Perakende Evrakı, Mâbeyn Erkânı ve Saray Görevlileri (Y.PRK.SGE).

b- Registers

1. Darbhane-i Âmire Defterleri (D.DRB.d).
   nr. 26, 46.

2. Hazine-i Hassa Defterleri (HH.d).
   nr. 716, 11710, 13914, 14162.

3. Yıldız Esas Evrakı Defterleri (Y.EE.d).
   nr. 36, 273, 944, 945.

B. **National Palaces Archive**

a- **Classification of Documents**
- Evrak I (E-I), Evrak II (E II).

b- **Classification of Registers**
nr. 26, 1815, 4680.

C. **National Palaces Caliph Abdülmecid Library**
K: 35-2.

D. **Topkapı Palace Museum Archive**
Defter Tasnifi (TSMA. d)
nr. 8075, 8218, 9988.

II- REFERENCE WORKS AND STUDIES

AÇBA, Harun, *Son Dönem Osmanlı Padişah Eşleri Kadınefendiler*, Profil Yayıncılık, İstanbul 2007.

AÇBA, Leyla, *Bir Çerkez Prensesinin Harem Hatıraları*, prep. Harun Açba, Leyla ile Mecnun Yayıncılık, İstanbul 2004.

ADIVAR, Halide Edip, *Memoirs of Halide Edib*, London, John Murray 1926.

AHMED CEVDET PAŞA, *Tezâkir, vol.* I-IV, prep. Cavit Baysun, Türk Tarih Kurumu, Ankara 1991.

AHMET VASIB EFENDİ, *Bir Şehzâdenin Hatıratı: Vatan ve Menfada Gördüklerim, İşittiklerim*, prep. Osman Selahattin Osmanoğlu, Yapı Kredi Yayınları, İstanbul 2004.

AKGÜNDÜZ, Ahmet, *İslâm Hukuku'nda Kölelik ve Cariyelik Müessesesi ve Harem*, Osmanlı Araştırmaları Vakfı, İstanbul 1995.

AKTAN, Ali, "XVII. Yüzyıl Kayseri Kadı Sicillerinde Bulunan Köle ve Cariyelerle İlgili Bazı Belgeler Üzerinde Bir Değerlendirme", *I. Kayseri ve Yöresi Tarih Sempozyumu Bildirileri (11-12 Nisan 1996)*, Erciyes Üniversitesi, Kayseri 1997, p. 13-20.

AKYILDIZ, Ali, *Mümin ve Müsrif Bir Padişah Kızı Refia Sultan*, Tarih Vakfı Yurt Yayınları, İstanbul 1998.

ALİ, Kevser Kâmil Salim Öğüt, "Çokevlilik", *DİA*, vol. VIII, Türkiye Diyanet Vakfı Yayınları, İstanbul 1993, p. 365-366.

ALİ SAİD, *Saray Hatıraları*, prep. Ahmed Nezih Galitekin, Nehir Yayınları, İstanbul 1994.

ALPKAYA, Gökçen "Kadınlar ve Köleler", *OTAM*, vol. I, Osmanlı Tarihi Araştırma ve Uygulama Merkezi, Ankara 1990, p. 1-10.

ARGIT, Betül İpşirli, "Üsküdar'ın Zenginliğinin Bir Farklı Yönü: Saraylı Cariyeler", *Üsküdar Sempozyumu, V- 1-5 Kasım 2007*, Üsküdar Belediyesi, İstanbul 2008, p. 438-444.

ARSAL, Sadri Maksudi, *Hukuk Tarihi Dersleri*, Ankara 1926.
ATÇIL, Abdurrahman, "Osmanlı Haremi'ne Dört Farklı Bakış", *Divân İlmi Araştırmalar*, P.15/2, Bilim ve Sanat Vakfı, İstanbul 2003, p. 247-258.
AYŞE OSMANOĞLU, *Babam Abdülhamid*, Selçuk Yayınları, İstanbul 1960.
AYVANSARAYİ (HAFIZ HÜSEYİN), *Hadîkatü'l-Cevâmi*, vol. I, İstanbul 1281/ 1864-65.
BALCI, Ramazan, *Sarayın Sırları*, Elit Kültür Yayınları, İstanbul 2007.
BARKAN, Ömer Lütfi, "Edirne Askerî Kasamsına Ait Tereke Defterleri (1545-1659)", *Türk Tarih Kurumu Belgeler Serisi*, Türk Tarih Kurumu, vol. III, Ankara 1964, p. 5-13.
BOBOVİUS, Albertus, *Albertus Bobovius ya da Santuri Ali Ufki Bey'in Anıları Topkapı Sarayı'nda Yaşam*, trans. Ali Berktay, Kitap Yayınevi, İstanbul 2002.
BOZKURT, Gülnihal, "Köle Ticaretinin Sona Erdirilmesi", *Osmanlı Tarihi Araştırma ve Uygulama Merkezi Dergisi (OTAM),* vol. I, Osmanlı Tarihi Araştırma ve Uygulama Merkezi, Ankara 1990, p. 45-77.
DAVİS, Fanny, *Osmanlı Hanımı*, trans. Bahar Tırnakçı, Yapı Kredi Yayınları, İstanbul 2009.
D'OHSSON, J. Mouradgea *Tableau general de l'Empire Ottoman*, 1222/1807, Firmin Didot Freres Editeurs, Paris 1824.
Dr. SPİTZER, "Harem'e İlk Giren Yabancı Doktor Olarak Gördüklerim", *Tarih Konuşuyor*, prep. Cemal Kutay, vol. III, İstanbul 1965.
Düstûr, I. Tertib, Mütemmim, İstanbul Başvekalet Neşriyat ve Müdevvenat Dairesi Müdürlüğü, 1289-1322.
Düstûr, II. Tertib, Matbaa-i Osmaniye, Dersaadet 1331.
ELLİSON, Grace, *An Englishwoman in a Turkish Harem*, London 1915.
ENGİN, Nihat, *Osmanlı Devletinde Kölelik*, Marmara Üniversitesi İlahiyat Fakültesi Vakfı, İstanbul 1998.
EVREN, Burçak -Dilek Girgin, *Osmanlı Kadını ve Yabancı Gezginler*, trans. Sevin Okyay, Ray Sigorta, İstanbul 1997.
FATMA, Aliye, *Osmanlı'da Kadın: Cariyelik, Çok eşlilik ve Moda*, prep. Orhan Sakin, Bizim Kitaplar, İstanbul 2009.
FENDOĞLU, Hasan Tahsin, *İslâm ve Osmanlı Hukukunda Kölelik ve Cariyelik*, Beyan Yayınları, İstanbul 1996.
FONTMAGNE, Durand De, La Baronne, *Kırım Harbi Sonrasında İstanbul*, trans. Gülçiçek Soytürk, Tercüman Gazetesi, İstanbul 1977.
FRANÇOİS PETİS DE LA CROİX, *Etat general de l'empire Ottoman*, I, Paris 1695.
FREELY, John, *İnside the Seraglio*, Penguin, London 1999.
GARDEY, L., *Voyage du Sultan Abdulaziz*, Wick et Rumébe, Constantinople 1865.

GERMANER, Semra-Zeynep İnankur, *Oryantalistlerin İstanbul'u,* Türkiye İş Bankası Yayınları, İstanbul 2002.

GÖKBİLGİN, Tayyib, *XV-XVI. Asırlarda Edirne ve Paşa Livası*, İstanbul Üniversitesi Edebiyat Fakültesi Yayınları, İstanbul 1952.

GÖNCÜ, Cengiz, "Dolmabahçe Sarayı Dekoratörü Charles P. Séchan", *Dolmabahçe Sarayı Dergisi*, vol. II-III, Milli Saraylar Daire Başkanlığı Yayınları, İstanbul 2000, p. 81-100.

GÖNCÜ, Cengiz- Serpil Çelik, "Arşiv Belgeleri Işığında Dolmabahçe Sarayı'nın Mekân İşlevleri, Bölümleri ve Plan Özellikleri", *Dolmabahçe Sarayı Dergisi*, vol. I, Milli Saraylar Daire Başkanlığı Yayınları, İstanbul 2003, p. 17-36.

HATHAWAY, Jane, *Osmanlı Mısır'ında Hane Politikaları: Kazdağlıların Yükselişi*, trans. Nalan Özsoy, İstanbul 2002.

HURŞİD PAŞA, "Cariyeler Hakkında", *Hayat Tarih Mecmuası (HTM)*, P. V, İstanbul 1965, p. 60-61.

İNAL, İbnül Emin Mahmud Kemâl, *Son Sadrazamlar*, Dergah Yayınları, vol. II, İstanbul 1982.

İNALCIK, Halil, *Osmanlı İmparatorluğu Klasik Çağ (1300-1600)*, trans. Ruşen Sezer, Yapı Kredi Yayınları, İstanbul 2006.

____________, *The Ottoman Empire: The Classical Age 1300-1600*, trans. VOL. İmber ve N. Itzkowitz, New York 1973.

İPŞİRLİ, Mehmet, "Harem", *Diyanet İslâm Ansiklopedisi (DİA)*, vol. XVI, Türkiye Diyanet Vakfı Yayınları, İstanbul 1997.

İRTEM, Süleyman Kani, *Bilinmeyen Abdülhamid: Hususî ve Siyasi Hayatı*, Temel Yayınları, İstanbul 2003.

Kânunnâme-i Âli Osman, prep. Abdülkadir Özcan, İstanbul Kitabevi, İstanbul 2003.

KAYA, Gülsen Sevinç - Leyla Ayhan Soylu, *Osmanlı Hanedanından Bir Ressam Abdülmecid Efendi*, Milli Saraylar Daire Başkanlığı Yayınları, Ankara 2004.

KAZICI, Ziya, *Osmanlı Devleti'nde Toplum Yapısı*, Bilge Yayıncılık, İstanbul 2003.

KOÇU, Reşad Ekrem, "Cariyeler", *İstanbul Ansiklopedisi*, vol. VI, İstanbul Ansiklopedisi ve Neşriyat, İstanbul 1963, p. 3382-3386.

________________, "Esir Hanı", *İstanbul Ansiklopedisi*, vol. X, İstanbul Ansiklopedisi ve Neşriyat, İstanbul 1971, p. 5276-78.

________________, *Aşık ve Şair Padişahlar*, Doğan Kitapçılık, İstanbul 1958.

KURT, Abdurrahman, *Bursa Sicillerine Göre Osmanlı Ailesi (1839-1876)*, Bursa Uludağ Üniversitesi Basımevi, Bursa 1998.

KÜÇÜKCAN, İlyas, *Nakoleia'dan Seyitgâzi'ye Seyyid Battal Gâzi ve Külliyesi*, Seyit Battal Gâzi Vakfı Yayınları, Eskişehir 2009.

LADY HORNBY, *Kırım Savaşı'nda İstanbul*, trans. Kerem Işık, Kitap Yayınevi, İstanbul 2007.
LADY MONTAGU, *Türkiye'den Mektuplar*, İstanbul Kitaplığı, İstanbul 1973.
LAMARTİN, Alphonse De, *Voyagee Orient*, vol. II, Paris 1865.
LEWİS, Reina, *Oryantalizmi Yeniden Düşünmek-Kadınlar, Seyahat ve Osmanlı Haremi*, Kapı Yayınları, İstanbul 2006.
LYBYER, Albert Howe, *Kanuni Sultan Süleyman Döneminde Osmanlı İmparatorluğu'nun Yönetimi*, trans. Seçkin Cılızoğlu, Süreç Yayıncılık, İstanbul 1987.
MAHMUD CELALEDDİN PAŞA, *Mir'ât-ı Hakikat, Tarihi Hakikatlerin Aynası*, prep. İsmet Miroğlu, İstanbul, 1983.
MEHMED MEMDUH, *Tanzimat'tan Meşrutiyet'e Mir'ât-ı Şuûnât*, Sadeleştiren: Hayati Develi, İstanbul 1990.
MELEK HANIM, *Haremden Mahrem Hatıralar*, trans. İsmail Yerguz, Oğlak Yayıncılık, İstanbul 1996.
MILLER, Barnette, *Beyond The Sublime Porte*, New Haven, Conn,1931.
MOLTKE, Helmuth Von *Türkiye Mektupları*, trans. Hayrullah Örs, Remzi Kitabevi, İstanbul 1969.
MURAD EFENDİ, *Türkiye Manzaraları*, trans. Alev Sunata Kırım, Kitap Yayınevi, İstanbul 2007.
NECİBOĞLU, Gülru, *15. ve 16. Yüzyılda Topkapı Sarayı*, Yapı Kredi Yayınları, İstanbul 2007.
Nokta, 2 Nisan 1989, p. 52-53.
OKANDAN, Recai G., *Umumi Amme Hukuku Dersleri*, İstanbul Üniversitesi Yayınları, İstanbul 1952.
ÖRİK, Nahit Sırrı, *Bilinmeyen Yaşamlarıyla Saraylılar*, prep. Alpay Kabacalı, Türkiye İş Bankası Yayınları, İstanbul 2002.
ÖRİKAĞASIZADE HASAN SIRRI BEY, *Sultan Abdülhamid Devri Hatıraları ve Saray İdaresi*, Dergah Yayınları, İstanbul 2007.
ÖZTUNCAY, Bahattin, *Dersaadet'in fotoğrafçıları: 19. yüzyıl İstanbul'unda fotoğraf: öncüler, stüdyolar, sanatçılar*, vol. I-II, Aygaz Yayınları, İstanbul 2003.
_________, *Hanedan ve Kamera*, Aygaz Yayınları, İstanbul 2010.
_________, *Hâtıra-i Uhuvvet Portre fotoğrafların cazibesi: 1846-1950*, Aygaz Yayınları, İstanbul 2005.
_________, *Vasilaki Kargopulo*, Birleşik Oksijen Sanayi, İstanbul 2000.
ÖZTÜRK, Said, "Osmanlı Toplumunda Çok Evliliğin Yeri", *Osmanlı*, vol. V, Ankara 1999, p. 409-418.
PAKALIN, Mehmed Zeki, *Osmanlı Tarih Deyimleri ve Terimleri Sözlüğü*, vol. I, Milli Eğitim Bakanlığı, Ankara 1983, p. 550-551.
PEÇEVÎ, *Tarih-i Peçevî*, vol. I-II, Matbaa-ı Âmire, İstanbul 1281-1284/1864-1867.
PEIRCE, Leslie P., *Harem-i Hümâyûn: Osmanlı İmparatorluğu'nda Hükümranlık ve Kadınlar*, trans. Ayşe

Berktay, Türkiye Ekonomik ve Toplumsal Tarih Vakfı, İstanbul 1996.
PENZER, N.M., *Harem*, trans. Doğan Şahin, Say Yayınları, İstanbul 2000.
SARICIK, Murat, *Batılı Kölelik Anlayışı Karşısında Osmanlı'da Kölelik, Cariyelik ve Harem*, Tuğra Ofset, Isparta 1999.
SAZ, Leyla, *Haremin İçyüzü*, Milliyet Yayınları, İstanbul 1974.
________, "Saray ve Harem Hatıraları", *Tarih Dergisi*, vol. II, İstanbul Üniversitesi Edebiyat Fakültesi Yayınları, İstanbul 1949, p. 509.
ŞADİYE OSMANOĞLU, *Hayatımın Acı ve Tatlı Günleri*, Bedir Yayınevi, İstanbul 1966.
________, "II. Abdülhamid Devrinde Harem Hayatı", *Hayat*, P. III, İstanbul 1963, p. 7-13.
TAVERNİER, J.B., *Topkapı Sarayı'nda Yaşam*, Çağdaş Yayınları, İstanbul 1984.
TERZİ, Arzu, *Saray Mücevher İktidar*, Timaş Yayınları, İstanbul 2010.
TOLEDANO, Ehud R., *Suskun ve Yokmuşçasına-İslâm Ortadoğusu'nda Kölelik Bağları*, İstanbul Bilgi Üniversitesi Yayınları, İstanbul 2010.
________, *Osmanlı Köle Ticareti 1840-1890*, trans. Y. Hakan Erdem, Tarih Vakfı Yurt Yayınları, İstanbul 1994.
TOTT, Baron De, *Memories sur les Turcs et les Tartares*, Paris 1785.
ULUÇAY, Çağatay, *Osmanlı Sultanlarına Aşk Mektupları*, Ufuk Yayınları, İstanbul 2001.
____________, "Bayezid II'nin Ailesi", *Tarih Dergisi*, vol. X, İstanbul 1959, p. 105-106.
____________, *Harem II*, Türk Tarih Kurumu Yayınları, Ankara 1992.
____________, *Harem'den Mektuplar*, İstanbul Vakit Matbaası, İstanbul 1956.
____________, *Padişahların Kadınları ve Kızları*, Türk Tarih Kurumu Yayınları, Ankara 1992.
UŞAKLIGİL, Halid Ziya, *Saray ve Ötesi*, vol. I, Hilmi Kitabevi, İstanbul 1941.
UZUNÇARŞILI, İsmail Hakkı, *Osmanlı Devleti'nin Saray Teşkilâtı*, Türk Tarih Kurumu Yayınları, Ankara 1945.
__________, *Osmanlı Devleti Teşkilâtına Medhal*, Türk Tarih Kurumu, Ankara 1941.
__________, *Mithat Paşa ve Yıldız Mahkemesi*, Türk Tarih Kurumu Yayınları, Ankara 1967.
ÜNÜVAR, Safiye, *Saray Hatıralarım*, Cağaloğlu Yayınevi, İstanbul 1964.
VAKA, Demetra (Mrs. Kenneth Brown), *Haremlik*, Boston and New York, Houghton 1909.
WHITE, Charles, *Three Years in Cosntantinople; or Domestic Manners of the Turks in 1844*, vol. I-III, London 1845.
YILDIRIM, Recep, *Önasya Tarih ve Uygarlıkları*, İzmir 1996.
YOUNG, George, *Corps de Droit Ottoman*, vol. II, Oxford University, Oxford 1905.

Pages 2-3 Painting
Henriette Browne,
The Arrival in the Harem, 1860,
detail, oil paint on canvas,
89 x 115.5 cm, (Oryantalistlerin İstanbulu, p. 171).

NATIONAL PALACES
Dolmabahçe Palace, Beşiktaş - İstanbul
Tel: 0212 236 90 00 pbx   www.millisaraylar.gov.tr